Sun-Sentinel

Unbelievable!

THE 2003 WORLD SERIES CHAMPION FLORIDA MARLINS

This book is available in quantity at special discounts for your group or organization.
For further information, contact:

Triumph Books
601 S. LaSalle St.
Suite 500
Chicago, Illinois 60605
Phone: (312) 939-3330
Fax: (312) 663-3557

Printed in the United States of America

Jack Says...

"Nobody gave us a chance to make it to the wild card; we did that. No one said we could . . . beat the Giants, we did that. We didn't have a chance against the Cubs with Kerry Wood and Prior. We accomplished that feat. . ."

"Hey, nobody expected us to be here. Let the pressure be on somebody else. We're gonna go out there and have fun. "

"We were on a mission since, I would say, the Philadelphia series when we were trying to qualify for the wild card. From that day on, we believed we could go to the World Series. It hasn't even sunk in yet that we won it."

Jack McKeon
Florida Marlins
Manager

CONTENTS

Unforgettable

It's like asking which was the best Beatles song, the scariest Stephen King novel, the most beautiful Picasso painting.

Which 2003 memory stands biggest for the Marlins?

Was it Pudge Rodriguez under a pile of Marlins, still holding the ball high, after tagging out San Francisco's season at home plate? Or was it Alex Gonzalez lining a ball to left field, in the only place it would miss the wall, to tie the World Series with a 12th-inning home run in Game 4?

Do you take Josh Beckett's two-hit masterpiece that turned the tide against the Cubs or his five-hit series-clincher against the Yankees? And don't forget his four-inning relief stint in Game 7 against Chicago when he retired 12 of 13 batters.

But maybe you're into the details more than the dramatics. Maybe you remember the most important pitches of the playoffs as those from Carl Pavano in relief. Bases loaded. One out. Marlins down 5-4 in Game 2 with the Giants having taken the first game and now looking to draw blood.

Pavano struck out the hot-hitting Edgardo Alfonzo, then retired Benito Santiago to keep the Marlins in the game, the series, the full October drama.

"The biggest seven pitches of my career," Pavano said.

Or maybe it was another reliever in a similar October situation. Maybe it was Braden Looper in extra innings against the Yankees. Bases loaded. One out. This was Game 4, with the Yankees up 2 games to 1, and everyone wondering if this was the end of the Marlins road. But Looper got out of the jam. Got the season revived. Got the game to Gonzalez's home run.

Dave Hyde

"The most exciting moment I've ever been in," Looper said.

Of course, maybe the biggest moment came long before any of this, when October wasn't even in view. General manager Larry Beinfest sat in his office with personnel chief Dan Jennings last January going over what free agents were still available. They noticed Rodriguez remained a free agent.

They already were at the budgeted payroll, but called owner Jeffrey Loria to see if the dollars could be stretched.

"We were building with pitching and defense," Beinfest remembered. "And here was a guy who fit into that perfectly."

Loria agreed to spend an extra $10 million — $7 million of it smartly deferred — if Rodriguez would come. They pressed the idea of playing near his Miami home. Loria even called Rodriguez on his 90-foot yacht to convince him.

"You won't regret it if you come," Loria said.

He came. He didn't regret it. No one did.

Or maybe the biggest moment was another Beinfest and Loria production. This was in May, with the Marlins struggling. The results in this result-oriented business weren't coming for Loria's friend and manager, Jeff Torborg. So out went Torborg. In came Jack McKeon in as bold a decision as the Marlins could make.

McKeon was "between jobs," as he put it, meaning he had been out of baseball for going on two seasons. He was on his couch in North Carolina. Suddenly, he was out of managerial mothballs and running the Marlins.

Torborg's style was everyone's favorite uncle. McKeon's style was different. He left the veterans alone, guys like Mike Lowell and Derrek Lee who he saw were professional. They did their work. They didn't need help.

October is for baseball celebrations, and the Marlins had more than anyone could have predicted. Here, closer Ugueth Urbina embraces Juan Pierre after another incredible Marlins victory over the Giants in the Divisional Series.

But if he saw a young player needing prodding, that his work ethic wasn't what was needed, he might say, "This ain't high school." The message was sent. The attitude on this team quickly changed, though it certainly was aided by several other front-office decisions.

The announcement to not trade Mike Lowell, when everyone was speculating where he would land? The trade for Ugueth Urbina when every contending team was looking for relief? The trade for Jeff Conine after Lowell broke his hand?

Or maybe it was the call-up of Dontrelle Willis, who won nine of his first 10 decisions when the season needed a spark, that was the most important moment of the year.

Others consider Lowell's home run to complete a comeback at Boston — one night after the Marlins gave up 10 runs before registering an out — as the biggest shot of the season.

Still others take the surprise package of Mike Mordecai's two home runs to end extra-inning affairs.

And then there was Jeff Conine's baseball decathlon — home run, impossible catch, throw out of a runner at home plate — that won a big night in wild-card rival Philadelphia.

See how hard it is to pick a moment? How a great season needs a treasure-box full of them?

It needs luck, too. That's just how it goes. So maybe the moment was against San Francisco when Jose Cruz Jr., a Gold Glove-caliber right fielder, dropped a simple fly ball to spark a game-winning rally.

"Nine-hundred-ninety-nine

Jack McKeon loves to give hitting instructions, even if he doesn't have everybody's complete attention.

times out of 1,000," Conine answered when asked how often that ball is caught.

Or maybe the biggest moment-was not even on the field but off it. Wrigley Field. Game 6. The Cubs are five outs from the National League pennant, Wrigley Field is partying and Fox television announcers are counting down the outs to a Chicago win.

Even Conine was thinking, "Well, it was a hell of a run."

Then Luis Castillo hits a ball down the left-field line. Several fans reach for it, as did Cubs left fielder Moises Alou. Steve Bartman — everyone came to know his name — was the unlucky fan destined to have the ball come closest to him.

He deflected the ball just as Alou jumped for it. Neither caught it. Castillo was alive. And so, instead of having the second out in the eighth inning, the Marlins were alive and rallied thanks to…

An error by Cubs shortstop Alex S. Gonzalez.

Maybe this is the biggest moment of the year. The shortstop with the fewest errors in the National League this season booted a double-play ball off the bat of Miguel Cabrera that would have ended the eighth inning. Instead, the Marlins scored eight runs for the win.

And advanced to the World Series.

And opened another drawer full of October heroes.

The best? Do you like *Let It Be* or *Norwegian Wood*, *The Shining* or *Carrie*, Pudge's catching, Beckett's pitching, Gonzalez's hitting, McKeon's hiring or …

Miguel Cabrera

Mike Lowell goes down with a broken hand after being hit by pitch in August; Marlins would get right back up in battle for a playoff spot.

Jeff Conine

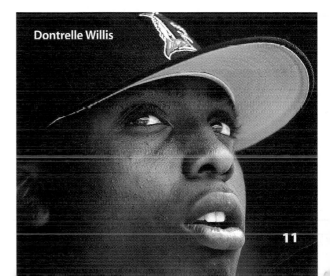

Dontrelle Willis

Hopes

You should be an optimist and have hope on Opening Day. You really should. You'll feel younger, look better and smile wider. Your pains will subside. Your personality will shine. You'll get 100 percent of the recommended allowance of vitamins just by drinking from a Marlins cup that's half full.

Anything should be possible on Opening Day. So what were the Marlins optimistic about on Opening Day, 2003?

That they'd have enough hot dogs, that's what. That they wouldn't run out of wieners and become a national joke, like they did one year earlier.

Sure enough, for the opener against Philadelphia on March 31, there were plenty of hot dogs. Fans even got coupons for free ones. A promise delivered.

As for anything else to look forward to for 2003 .....

"You want a prediction?" team President David Samson said. "OK, lets do it with some reasoning. Last year, A.J. [Burnett] and Brad [Penny] and Josh [Beckett] won what, 26 games combined? And we won 79 games. They're going to go up enough so that ....."

"I predict 91 wins."
Cough, cough.

Uh, 91 wins? Be a contender? Run with the biggest boys?

Well, isn't the opening of the season the time to hope? Even if there isn't much to hope for.

The Marlins were a franchise that could use a break. Everyone knows that. If it's not the owners who have deserted them, it's the fans. And if it's not the future that has been a nagging pain in recent years, it's the nagging pains that have been.

Beckett had blister problems throughout 2002. Penny went on the disabled list for six weeks. And they still won 79 games. And they did lead the major leagues with 177 steals, and figured to run even more in 2003.

Now, they had a bevy of young arms. They had $10 million free-agent catcher Pudge Rodriguez. They had speedy Juan Pierre, acquired in the off-season from the Colorado Rockies in a trade for Charles Johnson and Preston Wilson, and Luis Castillo at the top of the lineup. They were one-two in the major leagues in stolen bases in 2002.

Right fielder Juan Encar-nacion brought speed. Even Rodriguez, better known for throwing out base stealers, stole 25 bases in his 1999 MVP season. Imagine if Mike Lowell and Derrek Lee assemble a good season and not just a few good months.

"We're solid," manager Jeff Torborg said. "We're real solid.

"We've got to take chances. Just because we get thrown out and look bad sometimes and it takes us out of an inning, we can't stop."

Still, when club officials start tossing around predictions of 91 wins for a franchise that managed one winning season in its first 10 years, that's inviting derision.

"I really am excited about this club," Torborg said before the opener.

He talked about how he would sit in the dugout during spring training and think to himself, "Boy, is this an enjoyable team to watch." He talked about the Marlins' ability to "do the little things" and keep mistakes to a minimum.

Speed. Pitching. Offense. 91 wins (who was Samson kidding?). They talked about it all.

But other than the hot dogs, nobody could be sure of anything.

Who knew what awaited
23-year-old whirlwind Josh Beckett?

Pudge Rodriguez, the $10 million man, would become the heart and soul of the team.

A.J. Burnett, strong early in the year, missed most of the season with an elbow injury.

Lefthander
Mark Redman,
unhappy after
allowing an early-season
homer, turned into a
solid starter later.

Juan Pierre, dropping one down against the Padres, was among the major league leaders with 29 bunt hits.

Alex Gonzalez' strong arm and defense solidified the infield all year.

Grandpa Jack

Jack McKeon? Really? He's 72-years old! Did you hear that? He's 72!

"Age is just a number," McKeon kept saying during his first news conference on May 11 after taking over for Jeff Torborg, who was fired from an injury-riddled, 16-22 ballclub the night before.

If the firing of Torborg wasn't surprising, the move to hire McKeon was so surprising, so different, so utterly against the norm that it's, well, historic.

McKeon is not just thought to be the third-oldest coach in American pro sports history (behind baseball's Connie Mack and Casey Stengel). He's the oldest ever named to coach a team.

"Just being around these guys makes me feel 45," he said.

Sounds like a takeoff on the joke about how to feel younger and thinner: Surround yourself with older and fatter people.

McKeon wants his players to relax, have fun — "Winning is fun, and fun is winning," he said a couple times — and he does have a sense of humor. He once fired blanks at a minor-league player who ran a stop sign at third base. He traded his son-in-law from San Diego to Minnesota. And he worked for Reds owner Marge Schott,

which is sure to sharpen anyone's funny bone.

The big question remains: if what's good for McKeon is good for the Marlins, too. He has been out of the majors since managing Cincinnati in 2000. That's difficult to do in a time when ex-managers either land as scouts, in the front office or as paid second-guessers on ESPN.

The day before he was named manager, for instance, he had a typical day in Elon, N.C. He went to his 10-year-old grandson's baseball game. Then to his 16-year-old's practice. Then he did some gardening before plopping in front of the TV to watch a series of major league games.

"I didn't retire from baseball," he said. "I was just unemployed for a while."

No question the Marlins were struggling when Torborg was fired. Still, the move to McKeon was, well .....

"I thought they were joking," first baseman Derrek Lee said after being told of the change. "I'm still in shock. I didn't know it was coming. ..... I thought he was a new assistant or something."

Most players blamed themselves and the injuries to the starting pitchers, not Torborg, for the Marlins' 16-22 woes.

"It's obviously a shock. You heard the rumblings, but with three of your five starters down and we're not swinging the bat like we can, obviously someone's got to take the fall. And it's Jeff," utility player Andy Fox said. "As players we have to look and say, 'Hey, it's our fault.'

"Some of these guys in here, we ought to be sick to our stomachs after what happened."

General manager Larry Beinfest said McKeon was hired because of midseason jobs in turning around San Diego in 1988 and Cincinnati in 1998. No doubt that was part of it. No doubt it was because he was hired simply to manage to the end of the season, too.

You couldn't get the Marlins on this one for going the cheapest route, though. They're going to swallow $1.15 million owed Torborg and probably paid around another half-million to sign McKeon. So on some level this is about winning — and hoping an old dog can teach everyone some new tricks.

"I remember coming here in 2000 with Cincinnati and we thought this was an impressive team," McKeon said.

He had the rest of the season to try to turn the Marlins into that kind of team.

Jack McKeon, at 72, came back from retirement to manage the Marlins on May 11 after getting a call from Marlins owner Jeffrey Loria.

McKeon, coming out for an
encore after the Marlins ousted
the Giants, became the oldest
manager to win a World Series.

McKeon, a
grandfather,
encouraged the
young Marlins
to play loose
and have fun.

D-Train

You wonder why Dontrelle Willis smiles all the time? You wonder why he wasn't scared in his major league debut?

Maybe you should have been on Highway 101 in Palo Alto, Calif., back in early February. If you had seen his Mustang, overturned and crumpled by the side of the road, you would understand what makes Willis so joyful, so fearless, on the mound and everywhere else.

He had just dropped off his girlfriend and was heading home for lunch when a rear tire blew out. Going 65 mph on the four-lane road, Willis hit the guardrail and flipped his car five times.

Thankfully, he was wearing a seatbelt, from which he was able to unhook himself and wriggle out through the smashed rear window.

When the emergency crews arrived, Willis was standing by the wreckage, a little dazed but, incredibly, unhurt.

"He didn't even have a hair out of place," Joyce Harris was saying of her eldest son. "It was a miracle. It was the grace of God."

The trunk was smashed in so badly, Willis never got his compact discs. The only thing he retrieved was sitting in the back seat, as unharmed as the shaken driver.

A Bible.

No wonder Matt Sosnick, his agent and offseason housemate, says Willis approaches life with "tremendous gratitude."

No wonder Willis, before taking the mound each outing, takes a knee, says a silent prayer and points to the sky. He even does this before his bullpen sessions between starts.

Mike Berardino

"He deserves this," Harris said. "He's worked very hard to get here, but he knows he's blessed to be here."

Ten days or so after the accident, Willis reported to Jupiter for Marlins spring training and the final push on an amazing journey that culminated May 9 against Colorado. The lanky lefty tossed six strong innings, piled up seven strikeouts, and left with a 3-3 tie.

All in all, a pretty memorable debut for a 21-year-old making the jump from Double-A.

"Unreal," Willis said afterward.

Surprised? Maybe you should get up at 4 a.m. and follow his mom to work.

Harris, 45, has spent the past 12 years as a member of Ironworkers Local 378 in Alameda, Calif. She worked her way up from apprentice to crew forewoman and now pulls down $28 an hour.

The Four Seasons Hotel in downtown San Francisco stands 47 stories tall. Harris has been to the top, hanging outside in the wind, never even thinking of looking down.

"Sometimes we go up by elevator," she said. "Sometimes we use ladders. Sometimes it's a tower crane."

At its peak, the Golden Gate Bridge stands 746 feet above the San Francisco Bay. Harris has been up there, too.

Ask Willis where he got his funky delivery — all knees, elbows and what-in-the-heck? — and he'll credit his mom.

If Dontrelle ever starts taking himself too seriously or taking his gift for granted, all he has to do is think back to that morning on Highway 101.

"I think about it every day," he said. "Something like that happens, your point of view about everything changes. You start to appreciate things more.

"The people around you. Life itself. All of it."

Our appreciation of Dontrelle Willis has just begun.

Called up from the
Carolina Mudcats, Dontrelle Willis
brought excitement when he
made his Marlins debut on May 9.

After a 9-1 start, the second half of the season was an emotional roller coaster for Willis.

Pro Player Stadium attendance soared in the games Dontrelle pitched.

Willis ended the regular season 14-6, and was valuable coming out of the bullpen during the post-season.

Miguel Cabrera was brought up from Carolina in June, and the 20-year-old hit a game-winning homer in his debut.

The Kid

Miguel Cabrera reached the edge of the infield and kept jogging. He didn't stop until the only thing under him was green grass.

Not once did he envision his initial traipse into the majors taking him beyond the dirt. Yet here was Cabrera, who dreamed of following fellow Venezuelan countryman and shortstop Dave Concepcion's path, playing a strange position with a strange glove.

He looked as close to natural in his major league debut on June 20 as anyone with four games of left field experience could.

In his final at-bat, he was the Natural.

After going 0 for 4 with a strikeout and a double play, Cabrera filled the Marlins' left field production void with one swing against the Devil Rays. He crushed Al Levine's first offering over the center-field wall with a man on in the 11th to give the Marlins a 3-1 walk-off win.

"It's a special day for me," Cabrera said. "The first day I play in the big leagues and my first hit is a home run. I was 1 for 5, but that's fine."

A shortstop turned third baseman turned outfielder, Cabrera looked fine in left, catching all five fly balls hit to him without incident. He did so minus the benefit of any pregame work because of afternoon showers.

"It surprises me a lot," said Cabrera, promoted from Double-A Carolina to become the Marlins new starting left fielder. "I signed as a shortstop. All of a sudden I'm in left field. ... They brought me here to do a job, the same job I was doing at Double-A. I don't want to do more than I can."

Cabrera is so new to the position he still doesn't have his own outfielder's glove. He is using one that belongs to Mudcats teammate Chris Aguila.

At 20 years, 63 days, Cabrera was the second youngest player in franchise history to make his major league debut. Left-hander Felix Heredia (20 years, 52 days) still owns that distinction.

Nonetheless, Cabrera's arrival was considerably more trumpeted.

"With the hype he's gotten, it won't be easy," third base coach and fellow Venezuelan Ozzie Guillen said. "People are going to expect a lot out of him. People are going to forget he's 20 years old. I'm going to forget. He's in the big leagues and he has to produce. He's going to play with men now, not boys."

The addition of Cabrera into the lineup helped ratchet up the Marlins offense as the mid-season point approached.

With speedsters Juan Pierre and Luis Castillo in the top two spots of the lineup, the Marlins easily led the majors in stolen bases and pitchers and corner infielders must be on their toes expecting a bunt at any time.

There was power with Mike Lowell, Pudge Rodriguez, Derek Lee and Juan Encarnacion. And there was power *and* speed with Cabrera.

Some people called the attack "small ball." Whatever you called it, it worked.

"When I get a bunt hit, it's very satisfying because everyone knows you're probably going to bunt and I can still do it with the infield in," said Pierre, who led the National League with 24 bunt singles in 2002.

"You can't have home run hitters throughout your lineup," batting coach Bill Robinson said, "so you play little ball to let big ball happen."

"Baseball's a sport where the big man doesn't rule. As long as the little man has that stick in his hand and he does the right things with it, he's just as big as anybody in the game."

Right from the start, Miguel Cabrera was destined to be as big as anybody in the Marlins' lineup.

Versatility was Cabrera's trademark, as he played infield and outfield and brought a spark to a club that needed one.

Cabrera, who drove in
two runs against the
Giants with this
broken-bat hit, had
62 RBI in only 87 regular
season games.

Shown here missing a ball that Juan Pierre had called for, Cabrera made several rookie mistakes.

Cabrera, who had several key hits in the post-season, brought youthful enthusiasm to the club.

Pudge

The Marlins weren't distracted in their off-season pursuit of a 10-time All-Star nicknamed Pudge. Fresh off finishing second in their bid for pitcher Bartolo Colon, the Marlins noticed the best catcher in a generation remained unsigned less than a month before 2003 spring training.

Unable to attract a multiyear deal to his liking, Ivan Rodriguez considered the Marlins a worthwhile alternative. He signed a one-year contract for $10 million. More importantly, Rodriguez got to stay in South Florida, his adopted home, while proving he is healthy again.

His exploits are Hall of Fame-worthy. He won 10 consecutive Gold Gloves while with the Texas Rangers, largely because of his proficiency at throwing out base runners.

Thirteen seasons. Ten consecutive Gold Gloves. Ten consecutive All-Star selections. Three division titles in Texas. That American League Most Valuable Player Award in 1999.

And oh, that arm.

Since 1992, Rodriguez has posted the highest percentage of runners caught stealing six times.

From 1997-99, he averaged a 52.4 percent success rate.

"He might be the best ever throwing the ball," former Marlins manager Jeff Torborg said. "How can anybody throw harder and more accurately than he does?

"He gets his feet in position to throw quicker than anyone I've ever seen. The way he throws, it's kind of breathtaking if you're up close."

"I've seen catchers that threw the ball as hard," former Texas Manager Johnny Oates said. "Steve Yeager for example. I saw catchers who were as accurate. Johnny Bench was very accurate. Yeager was also very quick like Pudge, but I've never seen anyone else behind the plate that was quick and threw the ball with such velocity and such accuracy from any position on the field."

Added former general manager Doug Melvin: "I never saw anybody that came close to him."

When Rodriguez became a Marlin, his aim was pretty clear.

"My goal is to take the Florida Marlins to the playoffs," he said.

Maybe he tried too hard early in the season. His average hit a season-low .239 on May 30.

But he hit .367 in June, .376 in July, and .292 in August. As for his passion and his leadership, you couldn't put numbers on that.

"You're seeing real leadership what Pudge has meant to this ball club that hasn't come out," said Marlins manager Jack McKeon. "People look at the batting average and don't see the unselfishness that we see."

"That guy is pouring his heart and soul into this team," reliever Chad Fox said, after Rodriguez was ejected from a game for arguing with an umpire in August. "When you see him react the way he did, that sends a lot of excitement."

When third baseman Mike Lowell went out with a broken hand on Aug. 30, the team quickly signed former Marlin Jeff Conine to get veteran leadership and an offensive boost. It worked.

But it was Rodriguez who put the team on his back as the wild card race started to get serious.

"I know we need Mikey, but Mikey is hurt," Rodriguez said. "We just have to keep doing what we're doing, everybody doing their part. With this pitching staff we have, five runs is enough. If we keep doing this for 26 games more, we're going to be great."

"He makes a big difference," McKeon said of Rodriguez. "When he's hitting the ball he's a key guy in the lineup."

Rodriguez, who was ejected from three games, brought a fiery brand of leadership to the young Marlins.

After a jarring home-plate collision in the 8th inning of Game 4 against the Giants, Rodriguez celebrated after scoring the tie-breaking run.

Pudge shows off his dance moves with Derrek Lee after Marlins beat the Cubs in the NLCS opener.

A Higher Power was on Pudge's side after he ripped a ninth-inning single in Game 1 against the Cubs.

41

Wild!

On a night like this, after a series like this, during a September like this, the Marlins came running out of the dugout like children let out for recess and were hit by a noise like this that can heard all the way into October.

That's when their greatest accomplishment hit even them.

"In that weather, with the rain coming down, we could've had 10,000 fans," centerfielder Juan Pierre said. "Instead, did you see them?" The fans came in the rain. They kept coming, too. Some wore ponchos, some wore trash bags, some couldn't care less if they got wet. The fans were as ready for this 8-4 Marlins win over the Phillies as the team.

Do you see where this already has gone? Do you understand the surprise this team has accomplished?

It isn't just that it's won this season. That was unexpected. It isn't just that it sits at the doorstep of the playoffs. That was even more improbable.

But it's won back South Florida, too.

This is the franchise without a stadium, that baseball wanted to contract, that went through three owners in five years, that was blistered in print and radio,

Dave Hyde

that ran out of hot dogs and didn't have programs on an Opening Day, for heaven's sake. Everyone shrugged over its future and no one had a solution.

But there's a buzz about this team, a good buzz, and you heard it when Juan Encarnacion hit a three-run homer to swing open the game. He was met with a standing ovation from the crowd that actually could be called a crowd.

Left-fielder Jeff Conine made a running, jumping-into-the-wall catch and was met by a standing ovation from the crowd.

Juan Pierre became the first Marlin with 200 hits in a season, on a signature bunt no less. The crowd gave a standing ovation for Pierre until he doffed his cap at second base.

Brad Penny struck out Phillies slugger Jim Thome, for the third time in the game, and the crowd stood and cheered.

"That's the loudest I've heard it in Pro Player," said Penny, who has pitched here four seasons.

No one knows about their future. But they have a today. And a next week.

That's more than most teams in baseball can say. And here the fans come, growing bigger

by the night, from 25,311 on Tuesday to 28,520 on Wednesday to 31,935 on a rainy Thursday night.

The night began with rain on the field, ponchos in the stands and the equivalent of Fort Lauderdale beach dumped on the base paths in hopes of drying them up. Brad Penny slipped so badly throwing his first pitch that it didn't much matter it was a strike.

At some point in the fourth inning the rain stopped and, if the sun didn't come out, it felt that way in this stadium in this series in this remarkable September. With two outs in the ninth inning, the crowd stood as pinch-hitter Jason Michaels came to the plate.

"Nuh-nuh-nuh-nuh, hey-hey-hey, good-bye," the fans sang to the Phillies.

Michaels hit a ground ball to Luis Castillo, who threw to first. That was it. The sweep was complete. The champagne was loosening, just not yet loose.

But that wasn't the story this night. The story was more remarkable than winning. It was of being loved in return.

The author said there are no second acts in America. But he wrote that from another generation, back before seeing how many there are in love, in life and in the love of a baseball life as this Marlins season has shown us.

Mike Mordecai's walk-off homer on Aug. 13 against the Dodgers kept the Marlins in the wild card hunt as the stretch drive began.

43

If the Phillies had any chance of getting back into the wild card hunt, it was snuffed by this great catch by Jeff Conine.

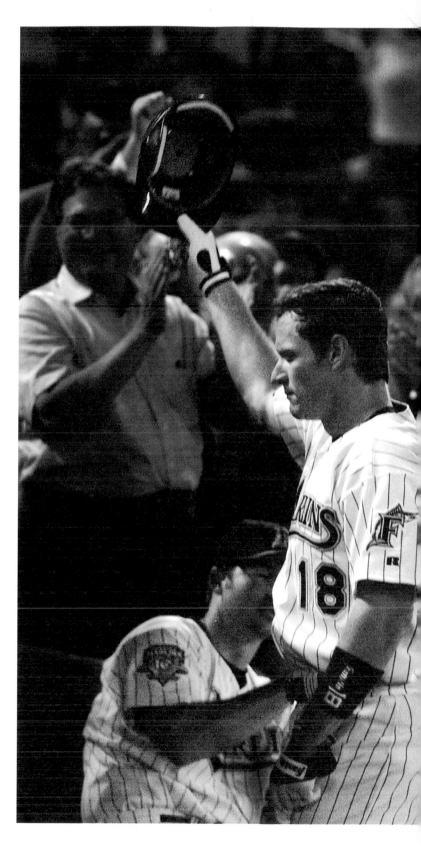

Mr. Marlin Jeff Conine, who had a spectacular series against the Phillies during the last week of the season, acknowledges the cheers after his sixth inning homer set up a 6-5 victory.

June Pierre celebrates after slapping a ninth inning single
to give the Marlins a 5-4 comeback victory over Atlanta.

It was unthinkable six months earlier, but on Sept. 26, Ugueth Urbina jumped into Pudge Rodriguez' arms as the Marlins clinched the wild card with a 4-3 win over the Mets.

Barry Who?

After the collision to win the game, Pudge Rodriguez held the baseball.

After the collision to celebrate the win, he held the baseball.

After he danced around the field, raised both arms to the crowd, gave a TV interview, screamed to the crowd, hugged some more teammates, danced again around the field, took off his chest protector, hugged some more teammates and finally began walking off the field, he still wouldn't let go.

"It's right here," he said. He took it from his glove. He flipped it in his hand. "I'm keeping it," he said.

So it was as remarkable to him - to all of them playing, really - as it was to all of us watching.

And how could it not be? Never in the history of baseball has a playoff series ended with the game-tying run being thrown out at home plate, according to the Elias Sports Bureau. But that's how the Marlins 7-6 Game 4 victory over the 100-win Giants ended.

When baseball historians look back at the drama-packed 2003 Marlins-Giants NL Division Series, they'll no doubt dwell on the heroics of Rodriguez and the gaffes committed by San Francisco outfielder Jose Cruz Jr. as the key reasons for Florida's upset win.

However, overlooking the unselfish and clutch contributions turned in by Marlins starter-turned-long reliever Carl Pavano would be a gross injustice.

Pavano, arguably the most consistent No. 5 starter in baseball this season, relieved in the final three games, notching wins in Games 2 and 4, while holding the Giants scoreless in the 10th inning of Friday's 4-3, 11-inning Game 3 victory.

"He never felt like it was a demotion," said set-up reliever Chad Fox. "You never heard him say, 'I should be starting.' He was pumped up about being down there and helping the team.

"That's what makes this team winners."

And then there was Barry Bonds, who almost turned into a mere mortal against the Marlins.

Bonds' seventh postseason appearance went more like his first five than last year's run to the World Series, when he hit .356 with eight home runs, 16 RBI, a .978 slugging percentage and .581 on-base percentage. Against the Marlins, Bonds hit .222 (2 for 9) with two RBI and had a .333 slugging percentage. He was walked eight times, six intentionally.

"I'm surely relieved, really. . . You know, I said I wasn't going to let him beat me," manager Jack McKeon said. "I'd be damned if I was going to let him beat me. [Edgardo] Alfonzo might have beaten me, but Bonds is not going to beat me."

Even with Bonds almost being a non-factor, it came down to that last play at the plate.

The Marlins lead had been cut to 7-6. Jeffrey Hammonds hit a soft liner to short left field. Jeff Conine could either dive for it or play it on the bounce.

"I wasn't going to dive," he said.

He fielded the bounce high, ready to throw. Which he did quickly and accurately. The night before, Conine crashed into the wall while catching a possible game-tilting home run. Now he was throwing to the plate. Lee, playing first base, kept his head down, not bearing to look, sure Snow would be safe.

"He threw the ball perfect on one bounce, and I caught it right in my chest," Rodriguez said. "I had time to put my right hand around it and hold on.'

"Throw the ball. Catch the ball."

"If you told me before the series that Jeff Conine would kill us with this defense, I would have said you were nuts," Aurilia said.

The same might have been said about people who said the Marlins would beat the Giants.

The great Barry Bonds was frustrated against the Marlins, getting only two RBI in the division series.

Juan Pierre is mobbed by teammates after scoring the winning run in a dramatic 11-inning Game 3 against the Giants.

Jeff Conine, who made several crucial defensive plays against the Giants, robs Rich Aurilia in the 7th inning of Game 3.

Oops! Jose Cruz Jr. drops an easy fly ball in the 11th inning of Game 3, paving the way for the Marlins' comeback victory.

The favored Giants are eliminated as Pudge holds onto the ball after a bone-crushing hit from J.T. Snow, ensuring a thrilling 7-6 Marlin victory.

One inning earlier, Rodriguez exulted after scoring the go-ahead run after another collision at the plate.

The champagne - actually the El Presidente beer - flowed over Alex Gonzalez' head as he and Luis Castillo enjoyed victory cigars after ousting San Francisco.

The Curse

No more bases to steal. No more runs to score. Yet here was Juan Pierre running as fast as he has this season.

He told people the Marlins were out to do the impossible, to shock the world. After the Game 7 victory over the Cubs to send the Marlins to the World Series, Pierre sprinted in from center field to celebrate that accomplishment.

Down 3-1 in the National League Championship Series, the Marlins completed their greatest comeback yet, beating the Cubs 9-6 in the decisive seventh game at Wrigley Field.

A standing-room-only crowd of 39,574 watched their beloved Cubs fall short of a World Series appearance for a 59th year. Instead, they witnessed original Marlin Jeff Conine squeeze the final out to clinch their second NL pennant in 11 years.

"I just had a bunch of fighting warriors that outplayed them," said Jack McKeon, who at 72 is the oldest first-time postseason manager.

Added Conine: "Heart. That's the only way to explain it."

Pitching on two days rest since throwing a complete-game shutout to send the series back to Chicago, right-hander Josh Beckett retired 12 of the 13 batters he faced from the fourth through eighth innings.

"There's no question [Beckett] turned this series around," McKeon said.

So many Marlins had a part in the unexpected Game 6 and Game 7 victories over Cub aces Mark Prior and Kerry Wood.

And maybe there was help from elsewhere.

If you listen carefully, you will hear footsteps stalking Chicago, as another generation of Cubs fans is linked with 1984 and 1969 and 1945.

Chicago led 3-0 in the eighth inning with one out and the Marlins' Juan Pierre on second base. Luis Castillo hit a foul ball down the left-field line. Chicago left fielder Moises Alou ran over to the brick wall, tracking the ball.

"I was saying, 'Don't catch it, don't catch it,'." Castillo remembered thinking. "But I thought it was a catch. I thought I was out."

At that point, the Marlins' season looked so buried it had moss growing over it.

Cubs starter Mark Prior was looking untouchable on the scoreboard. And with this second out, the lights were dimming.

"The way [Prior] was going, I thought, 'Hell, we gave it a great run,'." Conine admitted.

Do you believe in hexes? Because as Alou waited for the ball to come down, this twenty-something fan in a Cubs cap, Steve Bartman, reached for the foul ball, too. He got in Alou's way. He deflected the ball. Alou slapped his glove to the ground in frustration.

"It was a sign," Marlin Mike Mordecai said. "Like we just got an extra out here."

Castillo walked. Pudge Rodriguez singled to score Pierre. Cubs shortstop Alex Gonzalez booted a ground ball from Miguel Cabrera to load the bases. And then Derrek Lee, who entered the game hitting .136 in the playoffs, doubled in two runs to tie the score. And then Conine hit a sacrifice fly to bring in the winning run, Mordecai hit a three-run double and this game was done.

The next night, the Marlins trailed Kerry Wood 5-3. Didn't matter.

Cabrera and Pierre and Lee and everybody else started hitting, Beckett was overpowering, and the unbelievable had happened.

In the wild Marlins locker room after the Game 7 win, a half-dozen players uncorked bottles in both hands and proceeded to dump a Niagara of champagne on McKeon's head. He came up laughing. And crying, too.

"Can you believe this?" he said, trying to re-light his cigar. "If ever a team deserved this."

CHICAGO CUBS

Fans file into the bleacher entrance at Wrigley Field at the corner of Waveland and Sheffield before the start of Game 2.

Sammy Sosa and Pudge Rodriguez chat near the outfield ivy prior to Game 6.

Cubs manager Dusty Baker and of the Marlins' staff Andre Dawson share a moment before the start of the NLCS.

In the game that may have turned the playoffs around, Josh Beckett is excited after his two-hit shutout over the Cubs in Game 5.

Coming off the bench, Mike Lowell slammed a game-winning homer in the 11th inning of Game 1.

Reliever Braden Looper reacts after getting the final out of the Game 1 victory at Wrigley Field.

Things looked pretty bleak for the Marlins and Luis Castillo as the Cubs romped to a Game 4 victory and a 3-1 lead in the series.

Cubs third baseman Aramis
Ramirez watches the flight of his
first inning grand slam in Game 4,
starting an 8-3 Chicago victory

Dontrelle Willis
is frustrated
with himself
after giving up
the homer to
Aramis Ramirez
that put the
Marlins in a big
hole.

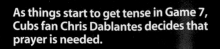
As things start to get tense in Game 7, Cubs fan Chris Dablantes decides that prayer is needed.

Mike Mordecai cracks the 8th inning double that helped put away the Cubs in Game 6, tying the series.

Not again! Cub fans think their team is cursed, and outfielder Moises Alou might have thought so, too, as he grimaces after a fan's interference kept the Marlins' rally alive.

As the Marlins celebrate winning the National League pennant, Cubs fan Wendy Diershow, 9, can only watch in sorrow.

Down 3 games to 1 and facing the end of the season, the Marlins beat the Cubs three straight, celebrating on the infield at Wrigley Field after the final out In Game 7.

Believe it!

The night was all done. The season was all won. Josh Beckett had the ball in his glove, just as he had the game all night, only now he was jumping with it on the foul side of the first-base line as Marlins players came running at him from the dugout, the outfield, maybe all the way from 1997.

Derrek Lee got to him first, smothering him in a hug. Pudge Rodriguez joined them, his catcher's mask already thrown to the skyline. Juan Pierre was sprinting in from center field, screaming all the way, then leaping into the kind of rush-hour scene New Yorkers expect on their streets but never on their infield. In Yankee Stadium.

Incredible.

Marl-in-credible.

"Oh, my god," Marlins owner Jeffrey Loria kept saying from his seat after this 2-0 Marlins victory in this stadium where he grew up as a kid watching games.

"Can you believe it?" Jack McKeon said as he walked out to the field.

Beckett was being lifted up on his teammates' shoulders now. Someone tugged a "World Champion Marlins" cap on his head backward. The caps were going on everyone, T-shirts, too. The phrase will take some

practice: World Champion Marlins. Read it again and weep a little, considering many of the Marlins were by now: World Champion Marlins.

From the contraction slab to a World Series Game 6 victory, the Marlins became the first visiting team to spill Series bubbly in the House that Ruth Built since the 1981 Los Angeles Dodgers.

"The way Beckett was pitching today, the way he was the last outing, they weren't going to hurt him," said shortstop Alex Gonzalez.

By now, the party in the clubhouse was rocking. The players took a chilled bottle of champagne as they walked in. The World Series trophy was being handed to Loria, the Most Valuable Player trophy to Beckett.

The music was firing up. Pierre and Dontrelle Willis were doing this dance they began doing before games in the summer. Gonzalez held up champagne and took a swig. Jeff Conine, the oldest and newest of the Marlins, was asked how it felt to run into that celebration in front of a silent Yankee Stadium.

"It seemed surreal to me to . . . " he said, interrupted by a steady spray of champagne into his face.

Conine opened his mouth.

"Damn, it tastes even better than the last time!" he said.

He was there in 1997. This felt different. This felt even better. This was a surprise season from the start to this happy ending, when on a surprisingly hospitable October evening, they leaned on Beckett's right arm and again on their playoff resourcefulness.

"It's like someone up above was script-writing every one of these games," Loria said.

What an October it was. What a ride they gave.

They won three extra-inning games.

They won three games they trailed by three or more runs.

They won four games in their final at-bat. They clinched series on the road at Wrigley Field and Yankee Stadium.

They won with their bullpen leaking oil, the batting lineup missing gears and a rookie deservedly in the cleanup spot.

And now, for one final snapshot moment, there was Loria running the bases in an empty Yankee Stadium. It was past midnight now. The crowd was all gone. The champagne was all sprayed.

And there was Loria sprinting like a kid again, jumping on home plate and being high-fived by his family. His smile was as big as this October surprise.

Prior to the start of Game 1 in Yankee Stadium, managers Jack McKeon and Joe Torre exchange war stories.

David Wells, bummed out after walking Jeff Conine in Game 1, was bummed out even more after leaving Game 5 with a back injury.

Nick Johnson finds out Pudge Rodriguez' arm is as good as advertised, after getting tagged out by Mike Lowell in Game 1.

The Yankees had the history, but the Marlins were the ones congratulating each other after 3-2 victory in Series opener.

Andy Pettitte pitched into the ninth inning while dominating in Game 2.

Josh Beckett, A.J. Burnett can only watch and try to stay warm as Yankees control Game 2.

PUDGE ZONE PUDGE ZONE PUDGE

NEW ERA CAP.COM NEW ERA C

Josh Beckett
acknowledges the cheers
from rain-soaked crowd
at Pro Player Stadium
during Game 3.

BECKETT
21

MARLINS
34

Derek Jeter, who had three hits in Game 3, slides safely into third base to set up a run.

Pudge Rodriguez walks off after being caught in run down during Game 3.

Every player's dream comes true for
Alex Gonzalez as he soars over
home plate and into his ecstatic
teammates after game-winning
homer in 12th inning of Game 4.

Roger Clemens, making the final start of his Hall of Fame career, tips his hat to the crowd after getting huge ovation after leaving Game 4.

There wasn't much to smile about for
Derek Jeter and his Yankee teammates
as the Marlins took control of the Series
with a 6-4 victory in Game 5.

Brad Penny won two games in the Series, and is totally pumped up after retiring Yankees in 7th inning of Game 5.

Yep, he touched it.
Alex Gonzalez gets a hand
on home plate ahead of
Jorge Posada's tag to score
crucial first run in fifth inning
of Game 6.

Josh Beckett gets the ride of a lifetime on his teammates' shoulders after dominating the Yankees and pitching the Marlins to the Series title.

MARLINS

Jeff Conine, who also played on the 1997 champion Marlins, gets to grasp the trophy again while getting a fully-clothed shower.

Dontrelle Willis and Juan Pierre, who typified the youth and exuberance of the Marlins, show off some of their best moves while celebrating the World Series title.

The Fans

So many players, so many comebacks, so many incredible moments were a part of the Marlins' 2003 championship season.

But almost as unbelievable as the Marlins were the fans. Yes, there are baseball fans in South Florida.

So many baseball fans, in fact, that 65,000 seats at every postseason game weren't enough. This from a team that averaged 16,000 per game during the regular season.

Before the start of the World Series, pandemonium prevailed at Pro Player Stadium, where about 3,000 fans converged for the 10 a.m. start of ticket sales. Early in the morning, team officials distributed 2,000 bright yellow wristbands ensuring fans would have the chance to buy up to six tickets each for each of the three home Series games against the Yankees. By 1 p.m., all tickets, prices ranging from $60 to $145, were sold.

About 17,000 tickets were sold in person at the souvenir store and stadium. Presuming people bought the six-ticket maximum for each of the three games, that means 1,000 people got tickets in person.

At the head of the line was Jessica Lopez, 22, of Davie. She waited 24 hours for her wristband, went home and slept a few hours, then returned to collect 18 choice seats. Combined value: more than $2,000.

"It's worth it; everything is worth it, especially when it comes to the Marlins," she said.

Peter Davidson of Boca Raton grabbed the last three seats available. "I just gave them my credit card and took what they handed me," he said.

Dedicated fans began queueing up the night before tickets went on sale at the Marlins en Miami store in Little Havana. Camping among them, with wheelchair and lapdog, was 86-year-old Laudelina Pedrosa.

"She wanted to make sure," Pedrosa's daughter Marta said. "She knows all the players' names, all their stats, everything. During the playoffs her blood pressure went up to 240 and fire rescue said she should go to the hospital, but she said, 'If I die after the game, call rescue'."

Even those who couldn't get tickets showed up at Pro Player Stadium just to soak up the atmosphere.

"People just want to hang around here and be part of it, even if it's not in the stadium," said Steve Zwicker of Miami.

It would have been a ticket-seller's market except for one detail: no sellers.

Yes, winning helps everyone get along, but so does a team that connects with the area's residents. Six of the Marlins' eight regular position players are from outside the United States. The Marlins give South Florida a way to cross cultural lines and make connections, said Carol Spring, executive director of a local civil rights agency.

"If you look at the stands, you'll see the census of South Florida," she said.

"It's very multinational," said Marlene Simpson, from Trinidad and Tobago. "And that's good for the area."

Fabio Andrade, a Colombian who founded the Americas Community Center, a social services agency based in Weston, said, "You go to a game and say, 'There's not as much difference between us.' It's another way for a person to understand that we're all the same."

Lawrence Livoti, a lifelong baseball fan who appreciates the nuances of baseball such as the fact Pro Player arranges the teams of its top-of-the-stadium flags in the order of the National League standings, said it has been an unforgettable year.

"I really feel like we're going out on a high note. . ." he said, before Game 5 of the World Series. "We're here, it's October, and we're living a dream we never thought we'd have."

Believe it. The dream lives.

The Marlin fans that found their way into Yankee Stadium for the Game 6 clincher get a joyous champagne shower from Mike Mordecai.

Theodore Giminez of Tamarac is a World Serious fan, for sure. Here, during Game 4 of the Series, he shows his loyalty to the team and in particular his fellow Venezuelan, Miguel Cabrera.

A final-week victory over the Phillies in the wild card showdown had Marlins fans thinking playoffs.

As Miguel Cabrera kissed one good-bye against Roger Clemens in Game 4 of the World Series, Marlin fans Curtis and Pacquita Newton share a smooch.

South Florida shows it can throw a championship-style bash, as tens of thousands of Marlins fans party hearty during a parade along Miami's Flagler Street to thank the team for the incredible memories.

The 2003 Florida Marlins End of Season Roster

MANAGER 15 - Jack McKeon

COACHES 67 - Pierre Arsenault, 47 - Jeff Cox, 23 - Doug Davis, 13 - Ozzie Guillen, 16 - Perry Hill, 28 - Bill Robinson, 26 - Wayne Rosenthal

PITCHERS 29 - Armando Almanza (DL), 21 - Josh Beckett, 31 - Toby Borland (DL), 40 - Nate Bump, 34 - A.J. Burnett (DL), 49 - Chad Fox, 38 - Rick Helling, 41 - Braden Looper, 39 - Blaine Neal, 56 - Kevin Olsen, 45 - Carl Pavano, 31 - Brad Penny, 57 - Tommy Phelps, 55 - Mark Redman, 91 - Tim Spooneybarger, 58 - Michael Tejera, 74 - Ugueth Urbina, 35 - Dontrelle Willis

CATCHERS 17 - Ramon Castro, 52 - Mark Redmond, 7 - Ivan Rodriguez

INFIELDERS 20 - Miguel Cabrera, 1 - Luis Castillo, 6 - Andy Fox, 11 - Alex Gonzalez, 10 - Lenny Harris, 12 - Mike Mordecai, 25 - Derrek Lee, 19 - Mike Lowell

OUTFIELDERS 22 - Brian Banks, 18 - Jeff Conine, 43 - Juan Encarnacion, 14 - Todd Hollandsworth, 9 - Juan Pierre, 4 - Gerald Williams

2003 Postseason Stats

MARLINS WORLD SERIES STATISTICS

BATTERS	AVG	AB	R	H	2B	3B	HR	RBI	BB	SO	SB	CS	E
Penny	.500	2	0	1	0	0	0	2	0	0	0	0	0
Conine	.333	21	4	7	1	0	0	3	2	0	0	0	0
Pierre	.333	21	2	7	2	0	0	3	5	2	1	1	0
A. Gonzalez	.273	22	3	6	2	0	1	2	0	7	0	1	0
I. Rodriguez	.273	22	2	6	2	0	0	1	1	4	0	0	0
Lowell	.217	23	1	5	1	0	0	2	2	3	0	0	0
DeLee	.208	24	2	5	0	0	0	2	1	7	0	0	1
J. Encarnacion	.182	11	1	2	0	0	0	1	1	5	0	0	0
Cabrera	.167	24	1	4	0	0	1	3	1	7	0	0	1
L. Castillo	.154	26	1	4	0	0	0	1	0	7	1	1	0
Beckett	.000	2	0	0	0	0	0	0	0	2	0	0	0
Hollandsworth	.000	2	0	0	0	0	0	0	0	1	0	0	0
Pavano	.000	2	0	0	0	0	0	0	0	1	0	0	0
Redmond	.000	1	0	0	0	0	0	0	0	0	0	0	0
TOTALS	**.232**	**203**	**17**	**47**	**8**	**0**	**2**	**17**	**14**	**48**	**2**	**3**	**2**

PITCHERS	W	L	ERA	G	GS	SV	IP	H	R	ER	HR	BB	SO
Willis	0	0	0.00	3	0	0	3.2	4	0	0	0	2	3
Pavano	0	0	1.00	2	1	0	9.0	8	1	1	0	1	6
Beckett	1	1	1.10	2	2	0	16.1	8	2	2	0	5	19
Penny	2	0	2.19	2	2	0	12.1	15	4	3	1	5	7
C. Fox	0	0	6.00	3	0	0	3.0	4	2	2	1	4	4
Urbina	0	0	6.00	3	0	2	3.0	2	2	2	0	3	2
Helling	0	0	6.75	1	0	0	2.2	2	2	2	1	0	2
Looper	1	0	9.82	4	0	0	3.2	6	4	4	2	0	4
Redman	0	1	15.43	1	1	0	2.3	5	4	4	1	2	2
TOTALS	**4**	**2**	**3.21**	**6**	**6**	**2**	**56.0**	**54**	**21**	**20**	**6**	**22**	**49**

MARLINS POSTSEASON STATISTICS

BATTERS	AVG	AB	R	H	2B	3B	HR	RBI	BB	SO	SB	CS	E
Willis	1.000	3	1	3	0	1	0	0	0	0	0	0	0
Hollandsworth	.500	8	3	4	1	0	0	2	1	3	0	0	0
Penny	.500	4	0	2	0	0	0	2	0	1	0	0	0
Conine	.440	50	10	22	2	1	1	5	9	5	0	0	1
Cabrera	.318	44	10	14	2	0	3	9	3	12	0	0	1
Rodriguez	.313	67	10	21	5	0	3	17	9	12	0	0	1
Pierre	.301	73	12	22	4	2	0	7	8	4	3	4	0
Harris	.250	4	0	1	0	0	0	1	0	0	0	0	0
Castillo	.211	71	6	15	4	0	0	4	8	12	3	1	0
Lee	.208	72	6	15	3	0	1	8	3	17	2	0	1
Mordecai	.200	5	1	1	1	0	0	3	0	0	0	0	0
Lowell	.196	46	6	9	1	0	2	5	5	8	0	0	0
Encarnacion	.184	38	3	7	1	0	2	3	3	12	0	0	0
Beckett	.182	11	0	2	0	0	0	0	0	6	0	0	0
Gonzalez	.161	62	6	10	4	0	1	6	1	16	0	1	2
Banks	.000	3	1	0	0	0	0	0	1	0	0	0	0
Helling	.000	1	0	0	0	0	0	0	0	0	0	0	0
Pavano	.000	4	0	0	0	0	0	0	0	2	0	0	0
Redman	.000	4	0	0	0	0	0	0	1	1	0	0	0
Redmond	.000	1	1	0	0	0	0	0	0	0	0	0	0
TOTALS	**.251**	**605**	**77**	**152**	**28**	**4**	**14**	**74**	**56**	**118**	**8**	**6**	**7**

PITCHERS	W	L	ERA	G	GS	SV	IP	H	R	ER	HR	BB	SO
Pavano	2	0	1.40	8	2	0	19.1	17	3	3	0	3	15
Beckett	2	2	2.11	6	5	0	42.2	21	10	10	3	12	47
Urbina	1	0	3.46	10	0	4	13.0	8	5	5	1	4	14
C. Fox	1	0	3.97	9	0	0	11.1	12	5	5	2	9	9
Looper	2	0	5.14	8	0	1	7.0	8	5	4	2	3	5
Penny	3	1	5.73	7	4	0	22.0	29	15	14	3	9	13
Bump	0	0	6.00	2	0	0	3.0	3	2	2	1	0	3
Redman	0	1	6.50	4	4	0	18.0	25	13	13	3	9	10
Tejera	0	1	6.76	2	0	0	1.1	2	1	1	0	0	1
Helling	0	0	7.27	4	0	0	8.2	11	8	7	3	6	7
Willis	0	1	8.53	7	2	0	12.2	15	12	12	1	10	10
TOTALS	**11**	**6**	**4.30**	**17**	**17**	**5**	**159**	**151**	**79**	**76**	**19**	**65**	**134**

Postseason Games

GAME	DATE	OPPONENT	SCORE	WIN	LOSS	RECAP
1.	9/30	@San Francisco	2-0		●	Beckett is sharp, but Jason Schmidt is dominating with 2-hitter
2.	10/1	@San Francisco	9-5	●		Juan Pierre goes 4-for-5, Fox and Pavano star in relief
3.	10/3	San Francisco	4-3 (11)	●		Pudge delivers dramatic game-winning 2-run single with two outs in 11th
4.	10/4	San Francisco	7-6	●		Wild finish as Pudge hangs onto Conine's throw to plate after collision with J.T. Snow
5.	10/7	@Chicago	9-8 (11)	●		Lowell blasts pinch-hit homer in 11th off Mark Guthrie
6.	10/8	@Chicago	12-3		●	Mammoth home run to center by Sosa highlights Cub rout
7.	10/10	Chicago	5-4 (11)		●	Glanville triples home Kenny Lofton for winning run in seesaw game
8.	10/11	Chicago	8-3		●	Aramis Ramirez blasts two homers, including first inning grand slam off Willis
9.	10/12	Chicago	4-0	●		Josh Beckett silences Cub bats with 2-hit, 11-strikeout complete game
10.	10/14	@Chicago	8-3	●		Marlins score 8 runs in 8th inning to beat Mark Prior and force deciding game
11.	10/15	@Chicago	9-6	●		Cabrera's early homer, Beckett's late relief beat Kerry Wood and send Marlins to Series
12.	10/18	@New York	3-2	●		Pierre and Castillo lead early small ball attack as Penny beats Wells
13.	10/19	@New York	6-1		●	Andy Pettitte stifles Fish as Hideki Matsui's early homer provides cushion
14.	10/21	New York	6-1		●	Following rain delay, Yankees score late to break open tight game
15.	10/22	New York	4-3 (12)	●		Yankees tie it in ninth, but Gonzalez' walk-off homer provides the real drama
16.	10/23	New York	6-4	●		Penny gets second victory of Series as Urbina barely holds on in ninth
17.	10/25	@New York	2-0	●		Pitching on 3 days rest, Beckett dominates and Marlins celebrate in Yankee Stadium infield

2003 Regular Season

GAME	DATE	OPPONENT	SCORE	WIN	LOSS	RECAP
1.	3/31	Philadelphia	8-5		●	Pudge homers, but early errors put Marlins into big hole
2.	4/2	Philadelphia	8-2		●	Mike Lieberthal's 3-run triple off Pavano breaks game open in 6th
3.	4/3	Philadelphia	8-3	●		Mark Redman strikes out career high 10; Encarnacion, Gonzalez and Lowell homer
4.	4/4	@Atlanta	12-7		●	Four Marlin homers, including two by Gonzalez, are wasted
5.	4/5	@Atlanta	17-1	●		Marlins belt three more homers, score nine runs off Greg Maddux
6.	4/6	@Atlanta	13-4		●	Braves score four runs in first inning as Penny falters
7.	4/7	@Atlanta	3-0		●	Sheffield, Chipper Jones and Andruw Jones hit three straight homers off Pavano
8.	4/8	New York	4-2		●	Redman lasts seven innings, but Al Leiter is too strong
9.	4/9	New York	3-2	●		Pudge gets game-winning hit, A.J. Burnett fires seven strong innings
10.	4/10	New York	4-3	●		Pierre's two-out single in the 9th is the game-winner
11.	4/11	Atlanta	7-4	●		Penny gets first victory of the year, and cracks first career homer
12.	4/12	Atlanta	12-5	●		Derrek Lee clouts two homers, including an inside-the-parker
13.	4/13	Atlanta	7-1		●	Lowell homers, but Maddux picks up first victory of the year
14.	4/14	@Philadelphia	5-2		●	Two-run double by Lowell provides early lead that doesn't hold up
15.	4/15	@Philadelphia	4-3		●	Jimmy Rollins' three-run homer in 7th is key to Phils' win
16.	4/16	@Philadelphia	3-1	●		Penny strikes out eight, Todd Hollandsworth has two hits, RBI
17.	4/17	@Philadelphia	7-3	●		Lowell's triple, Castillo's three hits make things easy for Pavano
18.	4/18	@New York	6-3		●	Tony Clark belts three-run pinch homer off Vladimir Nunez
19.	4/19	@New York	6-5	●		Castillo gets key hit in ninth inning as Fish come from behind
20.	4/20	@New York	7-4		●	Beckett is sharp for six innings, but bullpen gets rocked in 5-run Met 7th
21.	4/22	Milwaukee	4-2	●		Two-run homer by Pudge in 8th inning is the difference
22.	4/23	Milwaukee	5-4 (12)	●		Encarnacion's single drives home Castillo as Marlins rally late
23.	4/24	Milwaukee	4-2	●		Marlins top .500 for first time at 12-11
24.	4/25	St. Louis	9-2		●	Burnett walks six, Hollandsworth homers
25.	4/26	St. Louis	5-3	●		Lowell's home run sparks five-run rally in 7th
26.	4/27	St. Louis	7-6 (20)		●	Marlins rally for five runs in 9th, then lose longest game in team history
27.	4/28	@Arizona	7-1		●	Justin Wayne loses major league debut; Lowell raps three hits
28.	4/29	@Arizona	7-5		●	Three homers pace attack as Redman throws seven shutout innings
29.	4/30	@Arizona	7-3		●	Marlins fall behind 5-0 early, never threaten
30.	5/1	@Arizona	4-3	●		Brian Banks' first homer of the year breaks tie in the 8th
31.	5/2	@Houston	4-3		●	Two early homers and 3-0 lead aren't enough
32.	5/3	@Houston	5-2		●	Lee hits two homers, but Astros make early lead stand up
33.	5/4	@Houston	5-2		●	Astros complete sweep with three in the 8th off Spooneybarger
34.	5/6	San Francisco	4-2		●	Santiago's 8th-inning homer decisive in Marlins' fourth straight loss
35.	5/7	San Francisco	3-2		●	Beckett goes out after one inning with elbow stiffness
36.	5/8	San Francisco	3-2		●	Aurilia's single in 9th hands Fish sixth straight loss
37.	5/9	Colorado	5-4	●		Willis throws six innings in debut; Encarnacion hits walk-off homer
38.	5/10	Colorado	5-4		●	Hollandsworth has four hits as rally falls short in Jeff Torborg's last game
39.	5/11	Colorado	7-2	●		Castillo has four hits, including homer, in Jack McKeon's managerial debut
40.	5/12	@San Diego	6-1	●		Three more Castillo hits, Allen Levrault's first victory in two years
41.	5/13	@San Diego	6-5 (10)		●	Two Lowell homers aren't enough as Padres win it off Looper
42.	5/14	@San Diego	10-3	●		Willis gets first major league win as Lowell, Lee, Banks homer
43.	5/16	@Los Angeles	2-1		●	Pavano fires seven shutout innings, but Dodgers score two in the 8th
44.	5/17	@Los Angeles	4-1		●	Marlins' offense stifled by Odalis Perez
45.	5/18	@Los Angeles	2-1		●	Hideo Nomo stops Fish, who score one run for third straight game
46.	5/20	@Montreal	6-4		●	Willis takes first loss as Expos score four times in 4th
47.	5/21	@Montreal	7-2		●	Pierre has three hits and 19th stolen base, but Pavano is rocked
48.	5/22	@Montreal	8-2		●	Offense continues to falter as ex-Marlin Livan Hernandez wins
49.	5/23	@Cincinnati	8-4	●		Lowell homers and doubles; Marlins stop slump with five-run first
50.	5/24	@Cincinnati	5-4	●		Homer by Encarnacion backs Penny's pitching
51.	5/25	@Cincinnati	6-2	●		Marlins complete sweep behind Willis' eight shutout innings
52.	5/26	Montreal	5-1	●		Pavano hurls complete game 5-hitter as Fish streak reaches four
53.	5/28	Montreal	4-3	●		Spooneybarger strikes out five in 2.2 innings of relief
54.	5/28	Montreal	6-0	●		Michael Tejera's pitching leads to doubleheader sweep and six straight wins
55.	5/29	Montreal	3-2		●	Expos rally for three runs in 7th to end Fish winning streak
56.	5/30	Cincinnati	4-3 (11)		●	Griffey hits game-tying homer in 9th, and game-winning blast in 11th
57.	5/31	Cincinnati	3-2	●		Willis throws seven strong innings and blasts solo homer
58.	6/1	Cincinnati	9-6		●	Pavano gives up nine runs as Fish rally falls short
59.	6/3	Oakland	13-3	●		Two Lowell homers lead rout of Mark Mulder
60.	6/4	Oakland	6-5		●	A's score late off Spooneybarger after Fish rally from 5-1 deficit
61.	6/5	Oakland	2-0	●		Willis goes to 4-1 with seven shutout innings
62.	6/6	Anaheim	4-1	●		Homers by Gonzalez and Rodriguez back Pavano's strong pitching
63.	6/7	Anaheim	9-2		●	Garrett Anderson's three-run homer off Phelps starts Angels' rout

GAME	DATE	OPPONENT	SCORE	WIN	LOSS	RECAP
64.	6/8	Anaheim	8-5		●	Marlins lose early 5-1 lead as Penny is routed
65.	6/10	@Milwaukee	12-4	●		Four-run 1st inning, seven-run 9th highlight easy victory
66.	6/11	@Milwaukee	6-5	●		Castillo and Lee homer as early 4-0 lead stands up
67.	6/12	@Milwaukee	6-5		●	Brewers belt three homers, score five runs in 6th inning
68.	6/13	@Texas	8-0	●		Penny and Armando Almanza combine on a five-hitter
69.	6/14	@Texas	13-2		●	Rangers jump to 6-0 lead early and cruise
70.	6/15	@Texas	10-4	●		Redman pitches seven strong innings, Lowell homers twice to reach 21
71.	6/16	New York	1-0	●		Willis' fifth straight victory is a complete game one-hitter
72.	6/17	New York	5-0		●	Mets score four times in 9th to break open tight game
73.	6/18	New York	10-5		●	Mets jump off to 10-2 lead and coast behind Leiter
74.	6/19	New York	5-1	●		Tommy Phelps throws seven shutout innings, Lowell belts No. 22
75.	6/20	Tampa Bay	3-1 (11)	●		Miguel Cabrera hits walk-off homer in major league debut
76.	6/21	Tampa Bay	2-0 (5)	●		Willis goes to 7-1 in rain-shortened victory
77.	6/22	Tampa Bay	3-2	●		Cabrera triple, Lowell homer are only Marlin hits, but that's enough
78.	6/24	@New York	8-4	●		Castillo's two-run homer highlights four-run 6th
79.	6/25	@New York	6-3		●	Two early Marlin leads are wasted, despite Lowell's 24th
80.	6/26	@New York	6-1	●		Pudge hits single, double, triple; Willis goes to 8-1
81.	6/27	@Boston	25-8		●	Red Sox score 14 runs in 1st inning, 10 before one out is recorded
82.	6/28	@Boston	10-9	●		Lowell's two-run homer rallies Fish from 9-2 deficit for biggest comeback
83.	6/29	@Boston	11-7		●	Pierre has two hits, Lee homers, but Fish staff is pounded again
84.	6/30	Atlanta	8-1	●		Rodriguez hits three-run homer, Pierre steals three bases, Redman wins sixth
85.	7/1	Atlanta	20-1	●		Fish set single-game record for runs, hits (25) and margin of victory
86.	7/2	Atlanta	2-1		●	Rafael Furcal's homer in 13th beats Almanza
87.	7/4	@Philadelphia	2-1	●		Pavano bests Kevin Millwood in pitchers' duel
88.	7/5	@Philadelphia	5-4	●		Fish jump out to 5-1 lead, hold on as Looper gets 15th save
89.	7/6	@Philadelphia	6-3	●		Redman throws 140 pitches to complete sweep
90.	7/7	@Chicago	6-3		●	Ex-Marlin Matt Clement hits two-run double, gains sixth win
91.	7/8	@Chicago	4-3	●		Castillo, Rodriguez homers offset blast by Sosa
92.	7/9	@Chicago	5-1		●	Kerry Wood hurls complete game, Sosa homers off Pavano
93.	7/11	@Montreal	5-1	●		Hollandsworth's pinch homer, Encarnacion's single in ninth spark victory
94.	7/12	@Montreal	7-1		●	Expos score four runs in 1st off Redman
95.	7/13	@Montreal	11-4	●		Lowell hits No. 28, Pierre steals three bases, team is 49-46 at All-Star break
96.	7/18	Chicago	6-0	●		Redman, Urbina, Looper combine on five-hitter; Pierre steals No. 45
97.	7/19	Chicago	1-0		●	Kerry Wood outduels Brad Penny in front of 30,432 fans
98.	7/20	Chicago	16-2		●	Willis pounded for six runs in 3rd; Sosa homers
99.	7/21	Montreal	4-1	●		Beckett pitches seven shutout innings
100.	7/22	Montreal	9-1	●		Pavano fires complete-game four-hitter, Lee homers, Pierre steals No. 46
101.	7/23	@Atlanta	5-4 (12)	●		Mordecai homers in 12th after Braves rally for three runs in 9th
102.	7/24	@Atlanta	5-2		●	Cabrera hits fifth homer, Braves cruise behind Russ Ortiz
103.	7/25	Philadelphia	11-5	●		Marlins score eight runs in 8th to wipe out 4-3 deficit
104.	7/26	Philadelphia	10-5	●		Beckett strikes out nine, Marlins rap out 15 hits
105.	7/27	Philadelphia	7-6	●		Pierre's single in 9th keys comeback for sweep
106.	7/28	Arizona	3-2	●		Fish win fourth straight behind Redman's pitching, Cabrera's sixth homer
107.	7/29	Arizona	2-1	●		Penny fires seven strong innings, Looper gets 20th save
108.	7/30	Arizona	3-1	●		With 37,735 on hand at Pro Player, Willis beats Randy Johnson
109.	8/1	Houston	2-1		●	Six-game winning streak ends despite sharp outing by Beckett
110.	8/2	Houston	5-2	●		Pavano matches career high with eighth win; Lowell hits No. 30
111.	8/3	Houston	3-1		●	Astros bullpen stifles Fish; Pierre steals No. 53
112.	8/5	@St. Louis	4-0	●		Penny matches career high with 10th win, hurling seven shutout innings
113.	8/6	@St. Louis	7-3	●		Mike Lowell rips three hits, Willis goes to 11-2
114.	8/7	@St. Louis	3-0		●	Marlins can't solve Brett Tomko
115.	8/8	@Milwaukee	5-3	●		Pavano wins career-high ninth game, Encarnacion raps two-run homer
116.	8/9	@Milwaukee	7-1	●		Redman's eight strong innings, Lowell's three hits pave the way
117.	8/10	@Milwaukee	5-4		●	Brewers score twice in 7th inning to pin loss on Penny
118.	8/11	Los Angeles	9-3		●	Dodgers score six runs in 3rd to beat Willis; Castillo has two hits and stolen base
119.	8/12	Los Angeles	5-4 (13)	●		Reserve catcher Ramon Castro homers off Paul Shuey for walk-off victory
120.	8/13	Los Angeles	2-1 (11)	●		Fish get second walk-off homer in a row, as Mordecai goes deep in 11th
121.	8/14	Los Angeles	6-4		●	Redman drops to 10-6, Cabrera hits seventh homer in loss
122.	8/15	San Diego	10-0	●		Lowell hits No. 32, Penny goes seven scoreless innings for 11th victory
123.	8/16	San Diego	6-3	●		Marlins get four runs in 7th inning; bullpen sparkles
124.	8/17	San Diego	11-7	●		Beckett throws career-high eight innings as Marlins complete sweep
125.	8/19	@Colorado	10-2		●	Rockies rip Pavano and Almanza for easy victory
126.	8/20	@Colorado	9-3		●	Redman touched up for eight runs; Cabrera gets three hits
127.	8/21	@Colorado	5-4		●	Todd Helton's leadoff homer in 9th inning beats Looper
128.	8/22	@San Francisco	6-4		●	Giants score five runs in 6th inning, Willis drops to 11-4

GAME	DATE	OPPONENT	SCORE	WIN	LOSS	RECAP
2.					●	
30.				●		
3.					●	
32.					●	
33.					●	
3.				●		
3.				●		
3.				●		
3.				●		
3.					●	
3.				●		
0.				●		
.		)			●	
2.		)		●		
3.		)		●		
.				●		
.				●		
.				●		
.				●		
.				●		
.					●	
0.					●	
.				●		
2.					●	
3.					●	
.		)		●		
.					●	
.				●		
.				●		
.				●		
.				●		
0.				●		
.					●	
2.				●		

Unbelievable!

Project manager & design: Jeff Glick
Design: Tom Peyton
Editing: Gary Stein
Photo editing: George Wilson
Imaging: Diane Fitzpatrick
Research: Barbara Hijck
Marketing: Stacy Ostrau

Sun-Sentinel

Publisher: Bob Gremillion
General Manager: John McKeon
Editor: Earl Maucker
Managing Editor: Sharon Rosenhause

The accounts in this book are based on the reporting of Dave Hyde, Mike Berardino, Juan C. Rodriguez, Ethan J. Skolnick, Harvey Fialkov, Steve Gorten, Sarah Talalay, Nick Sortal, Robert Nolin and Gary Stein.

PHOTO CREDITS

Taimy Alvarez: 89
Robert Duyos: Cover, 3, 10(left), 13, 18, 19(top), 21, 23(top), 25, 28, 29(bottom), 30, 32-33, 34, 35(bottom), 37, 46-47, 54, 55, 56-57, 60, 61, 63(right), 64, 65, 66(bottom), 71, 72(top), 74, 75, 77(bottom), 79(right), 81, 85(top, bottom), 96
Michael Laughlin: Back cover, 4-5, 16-17, 26-27, 43, 88(top, bottom)
Melissa Lyttle: 7, 38-39, 52
Robert Mayer: 1, 8, 9, 10-11(top, bottom left), 14-15, 19(bottom), 22, 29(top), 35(right), 40-41, 44-45, 48-49, 51, 53(right top, bottom), 62, 66(top), 67, 68, 69, 72-73(bottom), 73(top), 76, 77(top), 78, 80(left), 82-83, 84, 87
Jim Rassol: 59
Susan Stocker: 90-91

Sun-Sentinel

TRIUMPH
BOOKS

601 South LaSalle Street
Chicago, Illinois 60605